As I Pirouette Away

Poems
by
Julie Chappell

Copyright © 2021 Julie Chappell
All Rights Reserved

Cover Image: *the dove is never free* by Steven Schroeder
Book Design: Rowan Kehn
ISBN: 978-1-7355762-3-7

Turning Plow Press
www.turningplowpress.com

For Hank Jones
who inspires, encourages, and believes
I can dance

Acknowledgments

I AM GRATEFUL TO THE FOLLOWING FOR INCLUDING MY POEMS IN THEIR COLLECTIONS:

"Disappeared" first appeared online in Laurence Musgrove's *Tejascovido*, March 26, 2020.

"Because It's Oklahoma," first published in *Bull Buffalo and Indian Paintbrush (The Poetry of Oklahoma)*, ed. Ron Wallace, TJMF Publishing, Clarksville, Indiana (2020).

"Symmetry," first published in *Speak Your Mind: Woody Guthrie Poets Celebrate Freedom of Speech 2019, Poems of Protest & Resistance*, ed. Dorothy Alexander, Cheyenne, OK and Santa Fe, NM: Village Books Press, 2019.

MANY THANKS TO THE ORGANIZERS AT THE FOLLOWING VENUES FOR INVITING ME TO READ MY POETRY:

Invited Poet. Original Poetry. "Helicopters, Butterflies, and Other Apparitions." Scissortail Creative Writing Festival Ada, Oklahoma. 2-4 April 2020 [Festival cancelled by Pandemic but recreated online as Scissortail Quarantine.]

Featured Poet. Original Poetry. Tidewater Winery, Drumright, Oklahoma, 10 November 2019.

Invited Poet. Original Poetry. Woody Guthrie Poets. Okemah, Oklahoma. 13 July 2019.

Invited Poet. Original Poetry. Bliss Books & Bindery. Stillwater, Oklahoma. 27 April 2019.

Invited Poet. Original Poetry. "Scorpion dreams among us." Scissortail Creative Writing Festival. East Central Oklahoma University, Ada, Oklahoma. 4-6 April 2019.

Invited Poet. Original Poetry. Woody Guthrie Poets Oklahoma City, Oklahoma. 13-July 2018.

Invited Poet. Original Poetry. "Cairns, Cigars, and the Blues." Scissortail Creative Writing Festival. East Central Oklahoma University, Ada, Oklahoma. 5-7 April, 2018.

SPECIAL THANKS TO STEVE OKA FOR HIS APRIL 2020 FACEBOOK POETRY PROMPTS INSPIRING BOTH "AUBADE TO SPIDERS" AND THE TITLE OF THIS COLLECTION

Praise for *As I Pirouette Away*

Throughout these pages, Julie Chappell weaves a rich tapestry of learning and longing. Everyday events that come into her purview bring to her brilliant mind insights that she sews like gemstones against a weft and warp of Virgil and Baudelaire, Gilgamesh and Ramses, Gregor Samsa and St. Antony. And the moments she recalls that ornament the cobweb mesh of memory and personal recollection are no less revelatory: "…in the mirror of your mind," she tells us, "you are what you ever were, / always trying to tease out your essence."
—Roy Beckemeyer, author of *Mouth Brimming Over*

Julie Chappell finds her poems in "the stillness of waiting" while "listening to the sounds of nature" for "the voices of time." And she's a damn good listener! She's got an ear to an astonishing array of interests: family and farm, Baudelaire, scorpions, a Carthusian monastery, Jimi Hendrix's "Purple Haze," lizards that grow new tails, Chaucer, Eliot, sewing baskets, and Paris. Chappell's pirouette of poems is rich with the simultaneous wonders of past, present, and future made known to us from her stillness of waiting.
—Paul Austin, author of *Notes on Hard Times*

This book is full of motion. Julie's keen eye catches life's little dramas occurring all around her solitude. Then, with intelligence and poetic composure, she turns inward, welcoming us into her memories— her courageous scrutiny of self and society confirming a sense of human decency.
—Ken Hada, author of *Sunlight & Cedar*

In her stunning new collection of poems in two parts, Julie Chappell's writing reflects human presence in the natural world and sets it to music with her words. In the first part, she finds beauty in the tiniest beings and most minute moments—a dragonfly, a bird dropping, a snowflake, a pelican, a soaring eagle, the wind on water. All become objects of focus and poetic elements. In the second part, she creates another view of life by combining her memories of lived experiences with her perceptions and imagination where she shows us the wisdom that comforts the soul. All of this proving that poetry (along with the devil) is found in the details.
—Dorothy Alexander, poet, memoirist, publisher
Village Books Press, Cheyenne, OK & Santa Fe, NM

Table of Contents

I - Helicopters, Butterflies, and Scorpion Dreams — 1
- Helicopters and butterflies — 2
- Butterflies are free — 3
- Pelican pilots — 4
- *Fortīs fortūna adiuvat* — 5
- Listening to Baudelaire on a winter morning — 6
- The storm — 7
- The way of all the Earth — 8
- In the stillness of waiting — 9
- Snowflake? — 10
- An aerial ballet — 11
- Gregor Samsa and me — 12
- Aubade to Spiders — 13
- Brain cells like lizards' tails — 14
- Ancient predator and prey — 16
- None shall pass — 17
- Scorpion dreams — 18
- The Battle of Qadesh, the Untold Story — 19
- Sanctity — 20
- Because it's Oklahoma — 21
- Neighbors — 22
- Resurrection — 23
- On the homefront — 24
- Nightmares floating in perfection — 25
- Dream on — 27
- Sideways walker and his cousin — 29
- The UnArtist — 30
- A flash of light in the darkness — 31

II - Memories Like Cobwebs 33

- The tease 34
- Purple haze all in my brain 35
- The family farm 36
- Symmetry 37
- Remnants of life on the plains 38
- Full of holes 39
- Forgive our trespasses 40
- Grandma's ghosts 42
- Grandma's sewing basket 43
- Keeping time 44
- Lessons my mother taught me 45
- Badges for my father 46
- My brother's blind salvation 47
- Talking Murder with My Brother 48
- *Disappeared* 49
- Cadence of the bells 50
- Pandemic March Blues 51
- Waiting redux 52
- Burning injustice 53
- Christmas Eve 2020 54
- Once upon a life 55
- Self- preservation 56
- Shadowboxing with cancer 57
- mæskə reɪd 58
- *Aprilis agon* 60

I

Helicopters, Butterflies, and Scorpion Dreams

For thurgh the word that he warp waxe forth bestes,
And al, at his wille, was wrought with a speche:
Dixit, et facta sunt et cetera
                    Piers Plowman, the A Text Passus X.33-35[1]

---

[1] Edited by Míceál F. Vaughan (*see Biblia Vulgata, Psalmi* 32:9; 148:5)

Helicopters and butterflies

The rumbling invaded the quiet
of placing books on shelves randomly,
as I, distracted, emptied bilious boxes.

Far from towns or busy roads
I crossed the floor to gaze
through glass heavenward

until

two helicopters invaded the sky,
their *whup whup* breaking
the still lake waters below them.

I stood staring, glass melting,
time dissolving into the *whup whup*
of death on nightly news decades before

until

scores of monarch butterflies filled the sky,
dispelling the real and imagined, soundless
in colors of autumn sunset,

a Requiem.

Butterflies are free[1]

Bare from the waist up, I reveled
in the freedom of solitude, of
warm sun and cool breeze on flesh,
when a butterfly landed on my shoulder.

Colorful and small, gently tickling
her flesh and mine as we
flew off together across
the bubbling, Blue Ridge stream.

---

[1] Apologies for the theft of this title from the film of the same name (1972).

Pelican pilots

Four white birds bounce along
on logs torn loose from shores
submerged by rain, wind, and waves—

Pelicans steering their wooden ships,
gliding, resting their wings, their spirits
for the long winter flight from ship to shore.

Fortīs fortūna adiuvat[1]

My fortunes fly fair today
seeing an eagle fly low,
head against the wind,
her wings flapping in the gale,
the lake rippling and roiling
beneath her flight.

Rarely but more often, I see her
flying effortlessly, swiftly
with the wind, gliding,
never flapping her wings,
the lake smooth, glasslike
beneath her flight.

She looked harried today
hurrying home to take her turn
sitting on the nest, perhaps,
warming the eggs beneath;
her mate in his turn to feed,
flying low with the wind at his back.

His return to her, too, will be fraught,
the wind in his face, as in hers,
until snuggled on the nest together,
warming their progeny-to-be
when the wind is warming,
and the lake mirrors their majesty.

---

[1] Fortune aids the brave. Originally from Terence's 161BCE Republican play, *Phormio* (I.4.26), repeated in some form or other by later Latin writers, e.g. Virgil's *Aeneid* (c. 19BCE) (X.284) where Virgil renders it, "Audentis fortuna juvat"—fortune aids the bold.

Listening to Baudelaire on a winter morning

Listening to a poet reading Baudelaire
on a podcast, I was beginning to embrace
Baudelaire's imperative, *Enivrez-vous,*
with poetry, not wine, for it was morning
in Oklahoma, not Paris. But, in the morning
in Oklahoma, the squirrels and birds were wild
with feeding frenzy, the birds swarming the
hanging feeders, the squirrels racing for peanuts
when suddenly, as if I were inebriated, my eyes
stumbled as a flash of white and brown came
swooping down upon a flash of rusty, bushy red
streaking away below the deck, into the trees.

The chase moving swiftly from branch to branch
until imperiled in the crook of one small tree, the hawk,
perhaps a Kestrel, struggled, caught by the tree.
I ran out with a drunken bellow, "Get out! Leave the
squirrels alone," following the now ascending hawk
with eyes and voice, as he gained altitude and equilibrium,
and I felt what? Motherly, because I feed the squirrels
peanuts each day so as not to feel so alone in these
woods? Or guilty, because I feed the squirrels each day,
setting them up for death? Or guilty, because I have
deprived the hawk of its feeding on a cold winter morning?

I stay out for awhile though soon return to retune myself to poetry,
finding it hard to concentrate on Baudelaire and his demand
that we get drunk on something—wine, poetry, virtue. Yet now,
I *am* hung over. The adrenalin of fight or flight of raptor and prey
infusing my blood, sending electric shocks through my being,
for my culpability in the tragedy of Nature's imperative.

The storm

In the storm, the wind chimes
make no sound even as they
sway east to west as if of a piece,
until the clapper violently careens
off one metal pipe then another.

The chiming notes resound but soon
are drowned by torrents of rain,
the cracks and roars of thunder
vanquishing their music in a flash.

While she sits inside watching, listening
for the comforting, transporting resonance of chimes,
she, too, is overcome by Nature's music,
the rain and thunder subduing, transforming
worry, grief, loneliness into an ancient tune.

The way of all the Earth[1]

The rust-colored squirrel sat
motionless, breathless after
the attack. The great hawk
unsuccessful, flying off portionless
taking a few turns in the sky
to regain his calm, his dignity.

The squirrel sat on, becoming one
with the bark, the brown leaves sheltering,
resisting their own death throes,
the tugging of the wind at their feet,
the squirrel's near-death encounter pulsating within
disproving his unnatural stillness without.

Me, watching from my window, helpless until,
running out to howl like a banshee at the departing
raptor, instinctively protecting the victim, while
riddled with guilt at having set the raptor's table
with squirrel-attracting peanuts, only to be left
aghast at the way of all the earth.

---

[1] 1 Kings 2:2

In the stillness of waiting

In the stillness of waiting,
the morning clouds dissipated,
drifted silently, patiently east,
the sun rising with the earth's tilt.

In the stillness of waiting,
the woods began moving,
singing, buzzing, skittering,
seeking first fruits.

In the stillness of waiting,
the child I was listened, searched
the sky, the forest, the ground,
untainted, innocent.

In the stillness of waiting,
arose voices long forgotten
and others sweetly familiar,
whispering, whistling, warning.

In the stillness of waiting,
I never saw the eagle long-looked-for
but other spirits emerging in
harmonic notes of waking life.

Snowflake?

On a cold, icing Oklahoma day
I cannot tell whether the heavy
white drop I just saw fall
was snowflake or bird dropping,
birds hopping on and off the deck
in frightened feeding frenzy in and
out of tree branches between which
that white drop plummeted, boulder-like
from branch to branch onto dead leaves.

An aerial ballet

Like tiny biplanes performing
at a fair, the dragonflies
swoop, spin, fly upside down,
twist, turn, and zigzag
to catch the even tinier insects
that pervade the air on this
lakeside, woodland morning.

I watch them and imagine
myself in another time at least a
decade after one war with still
a decade to go before another.
I am a child holding my mother's
hand gazing skyward at the aerial
acrobatics piloted not by
insect brain but human.

Biplanes swooping and spinning
bombing and firing at other humans
made war on each other, then the next war,
another, each deadlier than before
biplanes, fighters, bombers swooping,
spinning, turning the engines of war.

I reawaken to the dragonflies again
intent on their kills, but for survival,
not greed or conquest, not power,
simply sustenance to live another day.

Whose is the rational mind?
Whose the instinctual?
Whose shall prevail?

Gregor Samsa and me

This morning I killed a cockroach
with an apple core and thought of Kafka.
My cockroach had been perfectly docile,
domesticated, just like Gregor Samsa.
The night before he had been there swaying
gently to my music, scurrying as I approached.
Mistrusting his now uncockroach-like stillness
I bent down squinting to see if he was truly dead.

As I scooped up the flattened shell and guts with a
tissue-covered apple core, the instrument of his
undoing, his little brown legs, just like Gregor's,
wiggled slightly and then no more before I popped
the lot in the trash, oblivious of the Nature of my crime.

Aubade to Spiders

Morning comes filled with plaintiff cries from our cats. I resist as long as I can (my husband, an early riser, having escaped to his study while the cats still slept).

I get up, feed the cats, and then, bucket of peanuts in hand, slip quietly out the deck door to feed squirrels, titmice, jays, all the peanut lovers. But very soon, that routine will become more intense, more exact, more essential.

Spider season at the lake would be here now if not for climate change bouncing our temps from winter to spring and back again day to day. Once spring pushes in for good all the varieties of resident spiders in these woods will fill the deck in corners, across doors, between chairs and table, post to post each night to catch tasty insects, especially the tiny gnats that hang like droplets in the air.

I am grateful for the spiders' contribution to the ecology here and get to know them all, apologizing as I twist my broom around their intricate nets. Too often gnats, not yet consumed, escape for the day to become prey when darkness returns. With sadness for my sweeps, up and down and side to side, I pull down webs each morning, taking great care not to kill the builders in the process. Surely, part of our nest can be shared with part of theirs.

The spiders once webbed our doors shut before I learned to dance with them. Now, I move with care not only for the spiders' sakes but my own. A face full of web and arachnid is unpleasant for us both. I sigh at the thought of this spring, summer, and fall morning ballet, the spiders twirling webs as I pirouette away.

Brain cells like lizards' tails

Pencil to pad, I write *errors*
when my mind distinctly said *hours*.
I thought, is it a sign of dementia?
Or a cool, off rhyme?
Or the death of a brain cell?

If those brain cells were like lizards' tails—
the little reptile whose tail you stepped on
at the lake when you were young to stop it
running away when to your horror (and fascination)
the tail popped off, later it would regenerate—
that would be worth the momentary shock.

And *Errors* or *hours* wouldn't matter at all.

> They guard its gate, Scorpion-men
> Whose aura is frightful, and whose glance is death.
> Their terrifying mantles of radiance drape the mountains.
> They guard the sun at dawn and dusk—
> . . .
> A Scorpion-man shouted to his woman,
> 'Someone has come to us. His body is the flesh of gods.'
> The Scorpion-man's woman answered him,
> 'Two-thirds of him is divine, and one-third of him mortal.'
> *Epic of Gilgamesh* Tablet IX, Column ii (c. 2000BCE)[1]

---

[1] Trans. Stephanie Dalley. *Myths from Mesopotamia* (Oxford: Oxford U Press, 1998), 96.

Ancient predator and prey

For over 400 million years, the scorpion
has crept around this terrestrial globe
feeding, mating, stinging to survive.

The descendants of these ancient beings,
entering my house, built on the same globe
may not survive the curse that is humankind.

None shall pass

This sacred space of peace;
this sanctuary from everyday life,
this Paradiso has an Inferno.

No pope burns upside down,
no faithless float rejected,
no betrayer suffers mastication.

Just tiny, ancient inquisitors,
scuttling about, armed with poison
poised to pass harsh judgment.

Who blasphemes?
Who defiles sacred earth?
Who disturbs the Scorpion realm?

Scorpion dreams

I

Like a cockroach flies
buzzing in slanted trajectory,
the creature, not a cockroach,
bent its tail, flicked it, searching
for my flesh, my heat, my death.

I awoke in a sweat fumbling for light
something to dispel the image of
that moving thing, hell-bent,
whose ancestors guarded the gates
of Mashu where Shamash rose and set.

II

Like a bat, it screeched,
harsh scrapings vibrating my being,
the creature, not a bat,
bent its claw, flicked it, searching
for my flesh, my heat, my death.

I awoke trembling, crouching deeper
trying to shake the image of
that moving thing, hell-bent
whose ancestors craved immortality
from Utna the Faraway and then lost it.

> His Majesty said to his shield-bearer:
> "Stand firm, steady your heart shield-bearer!
> I will chase them as a falcon pounces,
> I will slaughter, butcher, fling to the ground.
>
> *The Poem of Pentaur* Papyrus Sallier III (c. 1273BCE)

The Battle of Qadesh, the Untold Story[1]

The sun-bronzed, god-assuming creature
they call Rameses, loudest, most reckless
most deadly in his disregard for all life,
raging here and there, shouting his lies.

We run, we burrow, we sting
panicking in our attempt to survive
rolling wheels, deadly equine hooves
smashing down among us,
arrogantly ignorant of our existence.

The noise subsides as both sides
retreat claiming glory and honor
while we who remain, sting as we go
through the bodies half crushed, breathing,
until we add one drop of our liquid death.

Then they know
who reigns truly in this desert
whose victory it is
whose truth should be etched
on those walls in place of the lies
of heroes conquered.

---

[1] The Battle of Qadesh (or Kadesh) took place in 1274BCE on the Orontes River near what is now the border of Lebanon and Syria between the forces of the Egyptian Pharaoh Rameses II and those of the Hittite Empire under Muwatalli II. After which, Rameses II boasts that his chariots defeated 3,500 chariots belonging to his adversary which he called *Aamu* to distinguish these "Asiatics" in the Syria-Palestine region from his Egyptians.

Sanctity

St. Antony alone in
the Egyptian desert,
save for us,
the scorpion men and women
who shared his fort
who danced round his consciousness
who kept our distance
from sanctity, holiness, the unwashed,
man unschooled in desert life
and death.

Athanasius told his tale,
but who will tell ours,
his first disciples?

Antony, overcome by demons,
his own lust and desire for
luxury lost and wealth relinquished,
went further into the desert—
few followed,
but we, his first disciples
who punished others with
stinging rebuke but let Antony
come and go from mountain to sea
from quiet seclusion to rebuke of heresies—
when he forgot us.

Until at the last, inside, alone,

save for us, his true disciples
stinging him with pure reason
steeped in poison no devil or god
could dispel.

Because it's Oklahoma

I

Because it's Oklahoma
and Spring
a warm breeze lifts the
tenacious, now-dried leaves
of the Blackjack trees with a
gentle lilting breeze that makes music
with the wind chimes, but soon will become
a raging thunderstorm running rivulets.

Disparate stones of earth eroding.

II

Because it's Oklahoma
and Spring
the scorpions have arisen
from their long winter lethargy
following the delectable spiders
and tender crawling insects
into tiny cracks in the walls and floors.

So far three have died in the attempt.

III

Because it's Oklahoma
and Spring
the rifts in the rocks, fissures in the earth,
ruins of human desire to drain the
red dirt of its oily wealth will bleed
every crawling thing, disturbed, disoriented
fierce with anger at their tormentors.

The aftermath will be terrible.

Neighbors

I live now in a woodland
of old and new growth trees
where my nearest neighbors,
scorpions, spiders, snakes,
and I abide in tense proximity,
not harmony nor antipathy,
coexisting as best we can
until one of us crosses the
natural DMZ of the other
and becomes fair game.

Resurrection

We consider cutting a path
through the trees
along the forest floor.

We assure the cosmos that

No trees will die in the attempt.
No rocks will be displaced.
No creatures will be annihilated.

But those crawling, slithering, spinning
may not survive our arrogant march,
to fulfill *our* desire for a little path

to take us closer to water from which
we crawled, slithered, and spun ourselves
millennia ago.

On the homefront

Every day I peer out through the trees
searching the ground, the skies
for a glimpse of the natural inhabitants
of my lake and forest home in Oklahoma,
and I imagine the scorpions, sitting patiently,
hiding under piles of rock or wood to wait
for insects, spiders, weaker scorpions
to cross their paths or come close enough
to be snatched in pincers firm
and stung till they can't squirm.

I once read that scorpions can survive
two years without food or water
which must be how they have outlasted
the onslaught of dangerous creatures
over millions of years, especially
the worst, the newest, the deadliest of all,
humankind.

Nightmares floating in perfection

The cat digs,
paws the floor,
pokes at the corner of
the cat bed near me.

Jumping out of my bed,
I put on the special shoes,
hurry to the spot, the cat
retreating, leaving it to me.

Flip the bed, nothing.
Lift the bed, nothing.
Move the bed, nothing.
Was the cat on nip?

Back to bed to attempt
to tempt sleep to me,
when another cat, vigilant,
plunges from his perch.

Out of bed again,
special shoes in hand,
Aha!

Scorpion cautious, unmoving.

I raise my weapon and
THWAP! THWAP!
twice deadly me,
dead scorpion.

The small scorpion body lay
oozing, flattened, yet intact,
still perfect in its symmetry,
the perfect little death machine.

A moment later, floating
in the clear bog water
the small body still perfect
swirls down to the Underworld.

Dream on

Abruptly stopped at the threshold,
the bathroom-bedroom borderland
where the dirt brown scorpion guards,
hoping to remain unchallenged,

I step down quickly; it
seems to evaporate beneath
the tread of my trainer;
the special shoes not yet donned.

No part of the creature appears
as I slowly lift my foot.
The full weight on one foot
crushing the floor but not him?

I search to no avail, shrug
and head to bed,
tired from the day
yet, sleep, now elusive.

Minutes pass in quiet until
one cat pushes, shoves something
no faux mouse this,
no piece of errant fuzz.

Up again, I shoo the cat away,
special shoe at the ready this time
to smash the dirt brown
body once more.

But something is not right
—pedipalps, cephalothorax,
metasomal segments intact but

telson, aculeus,
stinging tail bit,
deadly dart—
gone.

Sleep will not visit tonight,
only scorpion dreams with
scurrying dirt brown arthropods
and their deadly darts galore.

Sideways walker and his cousin

My son must have been about two
when I found the little crab scurrying
across our small apartment floor
after a day spent on the beach,
building rough sand castles,
searching for ghost shrimp bubbles
along the shore.

Displaced, the little crab scuttled sideways
frightened by the strange, faux sand beneath it.
My son, unabashed, showed me
his tiny pants cuff, full of real sand,
where the small crab had ridden, carried
lovingly home, where I scooped it up to return *it* home
along the shore.

This memory plays round my mind
when decades later I spy a relative
of my son's sideways walker,
another Euarthropode of softer shell
who needs no one to carry him to
the cool, dark corners of my home
where he can quietly wait for prey,
spiders, beetles, duller scorpions, my cats, me.

When he scuttles across the floor
I do not retrieve him, carry him lovingly
to return him to his log or brush pile home,
but ask forgiveness of the gods
and smash him flat.

The UnArtist

On the canvas of unpainted wall
the artificial glow illumined the ancient
stand off of Scorpion and Spider,
an unmoving tableau of death,
the first to flinch losing life or sustenance.

And I, Victor or Victim (only time will tell)
wield a weapon at the one I fear most,
yet only one will be vanquished.
Scorpion dies, and Spider waits.
Oblivious I, revel in short-lived triumph
while Spider slips away to rise again.

A flash of light in the darkness

The baby scorpion finds itself alone
when it wakes again with the darkness,
but it follows its hunger off the wood pile
and across a strangely hard ground, yet
it never falters, undisturbed by a wall,
neither rock nor wood, it climbs.

Halfway up it senses rather than sees
the spider, twice its size, and
the baby scorpion waits, motionless,
patient in its hunger.

Suddenly,

a flash of light startles the senses of
hunter and prey, stifles them both,
as the little scorpion feels a shock,
a collapsing of all its senses.

It falls from the wall, descending into
the realm of eternal darkness,
without dreams.

II

Memories Like Cobwebs

The blue carpet darkened a shade or two and the walls drew back into remoteness. The chairs filled with shadowy loungers. In the corners were memories like cobwebs.
                          "I'll be Waiting" Raymond Chandler (1939)

The tease

Teasing out a memory is not
unlike teasing your hair, after all,
you're back combing your mind
to find beauty in the tangles of
remembrance, pushing the strands of time
down, to the side, shifting the dander
of dissolution, dispersal, and death,
pulling out the shafts of sex, love, loss,
scrunching up the curls of karma,
enlightenment, and dead ends.
And, in one split end of recognition,
in the mirror of your mind you see
that you are what you ever were,
always trying to tease out your essence.

Purple haze all in my brain

The first time I heard Jimi Hendrix's
"Purple Haze," I was walking down a stairway
in an old, hippyfied Victorian house near campus.

Smoke of all varieties, thick and heavy, nearly blue
obscured the way down until the last step where
my foot touched the old, creaking wooden floor.

A room full of people lay ahead where Jesus, flowing hair
and all, sat with three women enrapt on a faded chintz couch.
JC was getting high and highly familiar with these women.

Mary, sister of James, Mary Magdalen, Mother Mary
come to me away from this manchild on a promise,
about to be one toke over the line, Sweet Jesus.

The family farm

The photograph, so aged and worn, has yellowed,
scotch tape holding the hay barn mute in the upper left
corner, blurred by tape but not obscured by time.
Two silos rise in the center above the milking barn
enclosed on all sides by fences and structures that,
like the tape, hold it all together.

On the right of the barn, cows mill about waiting their turn
while those already milked graze lazily in distant pastures.
On the left, internal fencing marks the spaces for bull and calves,
the bull's fence rising high behind his shed to keep his frenzy in
while a wider enclosure beyond creates a tiny lean-to for calves;
yet more fencing and outbuildings hold it all together.

Just beyond this, a sleek red chicken coop, a rock well house,
a tall, red horse barn, and cozy pig sty lay, and finally
the farmhouse stands, still, but rarely silent, foregrounded.
Here the men pass through to work unseen in those outdoor spaces.
Here the women, enclosed but not confined, labor to sustain them all.
Here chicken, pig, and cow become essential breakfast, dinner, supper.

Here men, women, and children settle in, content in their labors,
holding it all together.

Symmetry

I

A postcard sits on the desk where I write,
an aerial view of a Carthusian monastery nestled in
the hills of Yorkshire, c. 1398, sea mist daily caressing
the ruins of the life existing before greedy, grasping men
warred against it, letting scavenging minions send the monks
spiritually naked into the world while tearing down their walls
for power and profit.

Stone walls, whole and in pieces, crumbling, still bearing witness to
the silent labors of monks writing, translating, binding books,
weaving on giant looms, tending gardens, to nourish and heal,
no threat to anyone in their solitude, their contemplation and
now the wind through massive trees carries the chanting,
ghostly voices of erudite and earnest men done to death
for power and profit.

II

An aging black and white photograph sits opposite the postcard,
an aerial view of my grandfather's dairy farm in Kansas, c. 1944,
the shape of monastic spaces eerily echoed in farmer's enclosures,
now decimated by greedy, grasping men making a different kind
of war, tearing the lives apart of those who fed all hurting no one
innocent and hardworking farmers and families done to death
for power and profit.

The farmer's quiet labors lovingly given as the milking machines'
gentle *shahaha shahaha* softly careened through the air before
the cows he called by name were sent to pleasant pastures to graze
while the farmers and their families labored to bottle and can,
to carry the milk from family to family, sharing in the lean years,
giving to those who had mouths to feed, and nothing was done
for power and profit.

Remnants of life on the plains

Half walls of stone—fireplace,
kitchen, bedroom? Who tried?
Who died, defeated?
Square silo-like tower
half stone-half wood sits
derelict with the half house.
A solitary windmill alone
on the windswept plain lists
to one side, frail about to fall.
Once it was the core of
the farm's existence, its strength,
until drought or doubt arrived.

Full of holes

I thought of you as I do
each time I use this little
aluminum pan with tiny holes
punched out over the bottom
to make a collander. Not machine-made
but punched and molded by human
hands, my grandfather's, a neighbor,
an itinerant tinker?

When I thought of you today
I wondered if you could ever
have imagined that I would use
this to wash each piece of produce
during a worldwide pandemic.
I thought, "no," but then remembered
you had your own pandemic, when
your first babies were small, before
your youngest, my mother, was born.

1918 flu epidemic. Merciless. Worldwide.
Weakening. Ravaging. Killing families.
No vaccines to dull the fear or impart it.
Even on your farm, where your husband
transformed an old barn into your house.
Was he in the process that year? Did the worry
even touch you in the middle of the country?
In the middle of your life as you took this pan
full of holes into your hands to wash your fruit.

Forgive our trespasses

As I read a poet-friend's poem about the days
that he and his father trespassed on others' country
land to hunt and gather as all our forebears did to
find food, I think of that distant past when people
banded together to protect their own hunting and
gathering areas from incursions, trespasses of other
groups. Primitive times, we say, but the only difference
from then to now is the invention of ownership, the fence,
to control the wild aurochs, their descendants tamed, feeding us
their milk, their flesh, their hides, covering us head to foot.

My family owned land, raised the long since
domesticated Guernsey and Holsteins roaming
free within our fence, enjoying the creek that ran
naturally along the east side of the pasture, the shade
made by scores of trees, one so large that it once took a
small band of family and friends stretched fingertip
to fingertip to surround its girth. Like our ancient
ancestors, we burnt some of the wood of those trees
out in *our* field, to roast meats from *our* pigs, and
drink the cool water of the natural stream on *our* land.

When I was about 12, I remember my mother's righteous anger
when we caught two children, about my age, preparing to
climb over our fence one afternoon. My mother stopped
the car to chastise them for their arrogant trespass.
They had the audacity of youth to challenge her right
to her ancestral land, to a hundred years of nurturing there.
Yet her care that day was not the trespass of her ownership
but the potential danger from what awaited them on that
land, leading their group to threaten, to punish her family if
those children were injured or killed as they roamed the pasture.
What if they encounter your uncle's Holstein bull and get
trampled? Or if they drown in the creek? Or run across the
many copperheads that lurk in the grass? Or worse?

That same year, the city was encroaching on our borders
threatening tax beyond our capacity so we sold that land.
Developers divided it carefully into the smallest pieces to
give other groups the right to hunt, to gather, to forge the creek.
But when the bottom land flooded, as we knew it would, and
they cut down all the trees, killed off the water creatures in the
creek, and turned its clear, rippling waters to sewer scum,
we cried for our loss and theirs.

What will future archaeologists discover here when
we are all dust and mouldy bone? When they uncover
a shadow of a fencepost, skeletons of crawdads and
snapping turtles in a layer of ancient creek mud?
Will they get the story straight? Will they romanticize or
rationalize the dead creek, the bones they find there
as they trespass on our past?

et dimitte nobis debita nostra sicut et nos dimittimus debitoribus nostris.

Grandma's ghosts

Grandma's stories filled my child imaginings
not with fairies and magic but with real people
struggling in darkness stifled by breathless hauntings.

Always cemeteries were entered in fading light,
cold, ghostly winds flung doors wide, in
the opaque darkness of a Swedish winter.

Eyes wide, I listened mesmerized, terrified,
her eyes sly, watching mine, waiting
for the reaction she depended on for life.

As our imaginations wandered far away,
trapped in her wheelchair, unable to walk
she could only share the darkness of fading life.

Grandma's sewing basket

Grandma's wicker sewing basket sits silent
next to the desk at which I write. Its
brown wicker weaving faded and worn, the
wicker swirls, like gargoyles on a cathedral,
standing guard beneath the basket top, seemingly
immune to time, use and abuse, seemingly mute.

But this inanimate basket reminds me daily of family,
of Grandma, matriarch and arbiter, taking sides, passing judgment
though bound in her wicker throne, a wheelchair, intricately woven
with wooden arms and rubber wheels, allowing her to hold court,
hear the trials and tribulations of all and be wherever needed, this
sewing basket beside her wicker chair, holding balls of thread,
crochet needles, rick-rack packets, satin trimming, pencils for her
ever-present crossword puzzles or the daily diary book, residents
of the open compartment at the base formed by a wicker fence
connecting all four long legs, making the whole more stand than basket.

When Grandma's sewing basket came to me, no maker of material culture,
it became plant stand, phone stand, night stand, the basket filled with
seed packets, phone books, novels, notepads, pencils, address books, moving
back and forth across the country, city, or state never far from my daily life.
And now, Grandma's sewing basket stands a reservoir for half-used writer's
notebooks, prayer flags unfurled, a ribbon from a child's gift, and four of
Grandma's daily diaries, filled with revelations from my childhood, giving
voice to Grandma's sewing basket to tell tales of family tragedy, trauma,
unfulfilled potential, overachieving, sins of commission, sins of omission,
secrets and lies, the Seven Vices and Virtues of family.

Keeping time

My grandmother kept track of time as she
made daily entries in a cheaply bound diary,
a freebie from a bank, a funeral home, both
hoping for her business one day or the next,
her decades of being a farmer's wife never
leaving her even in old age, after the loss of husband,
babies, parents, friends, my grandmother keeping time,
recording for posterity our better angels, our natural devils.

I read her words now, long after losing her and others
whose names and deeds time cannot erase from this book,
a comfort in this age tracking time by cases of disease
of fear, of loneliness, of despair of death after death.
In her diary I retreat momentarily from this awful present
to live again a child's life where the greatest fears were
of monsters and hobgoblins, of foulplay in the school yard,
of brother's teasing tortures, of being alone in the dark,
as my grandmother counsels and consoles us all, and
like a creature trapped in amber, the golden glow of my
grandmother's wise, biased, and judgmental rendering
keeps the joys and sorrows of childhood tangible and timeless.

Lessons my mother taught me

When I was baking for the first time,
my mother taught me to use only deep yellow
egg yolks rising up above the curling white
and only be wary of ones colorless and concave.

When I was frightened by storm clouds
gathering above the Kansas plains,
my mother taught me to watch the cattle
and only be wary if they crowded in together.

When I felt my first pains of love and asked
her how I would know if it were true,
my mother taught me to search my heart
and only be wary of fairy tale deceptions.

When I had my first child and hovered too close,
fretting that I would not know what to do,
my mother taught me how to balance that love
and only be wary of leaning too far in or too far out.

When she lay dying in a hospital bed,
my mother taught me that I would bear eternal grief
for all that she could no longer teach me
and only be wary if her lessons died with her.

Badges for my father

Countless hours smiling, sharing
your love of human interaction
even the simplest kind with a new
badge for which you gave chits,
made change, offered directions.

But that badge left you in the margins
of a life you once lived, of service
to all, *that* badge had declared your worth.
The new badge proclaimed you just
another squirrel frantically moving the wheel.

Child of a world that promised
opportunity for all, if you only—
worked hard, pursued your dreams—
rewards would come. But your dreams,
your rewards faded long before you did.

My brother's blind salvation

His blind eye shrouded with scar tissue saved him.
But *he* thought it savaged his manhood beyond repair,
war raging, friends suffering, dying, and he, barely a man
stuck at home to fight against his working class poverty,
to ignore the salvation of education, to marry too young,
to carry no visible scars of his generation's war,
to be left behind with his one good eye,
a statistic ignored in the politicians' number games.

Talking Murder with My Brother

"Do you remember the murder of a woman in the late 1950s who was..."

"Beaten to death with a hammer? Maude Smith."

"That's right. I found pictures in Dad's desk drawer. Grisly, graphic. Dad told me the story when he caught me snooping."

"Do you remember the KU student who murdered his family?"

"Yes! Lowell Lee Andrews. A soft, fat, man-boy, who snapped on Thanksgiving night."

"Dad was sheriff when it happened, late 1958, got involved locally. Andrews was already on death row when Hickok and Smith joined him there."

"Oh, yeah, according to Dad, Hickok and Smith were remorseless, cold blooded. Do you remember the hammer murderer's name?"

"No."

"Me, neither."

"O.K., bye."

Just two cop's kids reminiscing.

Disappeared

I must have been about 3 or 4 when,
one day, I stepped silently between
a china cabinet and another tall piece
and *disappeared*, uncharacteristically quiet,
as I waited and watched my parents, first,
call my name, then, still calling, move
frantically downstairs, upstairs, outside,
searching for their lost child, while I calculated
the precise moment to appear, out of thin air
to be embraced, cherished, loved at last.

That memory came unbidden to me a few
days ago while I sat staring, not mindless,
but unfocused, waiting, watching life as usual
outside my window, the movement of Nature
as it unveils this year's Spring colors and critters,
all the forest striving in fraught, anxious beats,
while I wait and watch in fraught, anxious beats,
disappeared, testing not the limits of love
but of human arrogance and Nature's revenge.

Cadence of the bells

The deep, resonant tones of the buoy bell echoed
gently, soothingly by the cadence of the carillon bells
following on a more-than-breezy October morning,
transporting sounds of distant places, savoured spaces.

The sweet scent of kelp growing lushly in the Pacific
where my then very young children ran along the sand
popping the "bubbles" on the stem of kelp washing up on shore,
the hefty wind off the water, salty and thrilling.

Alone on a Sunday morning in Oxford the church bells
chiming, I wandered in the mist, aimless but not pointless,
simply without destination, libraries and archives closed,
the breeze off the streets stirring the past all around me.

The buoy bell and the carillon carry me along farther
from this place where we remain isolated for months
as the pandemic rages, debilitates, kills without moral center
or purpose beyond replicating itself endlessly.

The maskless hordes aiding and abetting its growth
following empty sound bites destined for their shallow ears
their angry minds pointing at someone, anyone but themselves
wrapped in the noise of a morally unfettered man, bleating.

Pandemic March Blues

We waited over two weeks after our last venture
before we knew to shut down for the long haul and
because I am vulnerable, my husband has gone for essentials.
He reports,
"You wouldn't know anything unusual is happening!
It's business-as-usual in the shops in Sand Springs."
His voice is bemused but not surprised.

I wait anxiously now calculating the time
when symptoms might appear and, what then?
Certain death for me but surely not for him?
He has to live to care for our cats who've been
confined to the house their whole lives with only
sniffs and glimpses through screen and glass.
I argued that I kept them safe from humans and
other creatures bent on their demise.

But humans are always every creatures'
worst enemy. Even their own.

Waiting redux

I used to keep a journal in my car
so I could write when I was waiting,
for children to come out of school,
for a store to open, the rain to stop.

Growing up with agèd grandparents, I began
at 20, in spite of a fit, firm, healthy mind and body
to wait for the inevitable fading—enfeebled, wrinkled,
ignored, infantilized. It terrified me then. Now,

my youth spent like easy money, I wait for an ending,
as disease multiplies, waiting in the shadows, in the air,
as cancer creeps, waiting to gain purchase on weakness,
as death beckons waiting to cash in on abuses of our youth.

Burning injustice

Notre-Dame is burning.
850 years of the sacred and profane
collapsing from human error, they say,
but isn't it always?

Alexandria, burning, untold words in flames,
pages of ancient wisdom, biting satire,
inscribed on the skins of beasts defenseless,
never to be recovered but yet, the story is told.

Roncevalles, boys with the baggage, soldiers, priests
perishing in the mountain pass, trapped by Roland's
youth and arrogance, needing to prove himself
to the Emperor who marched on, not looking back.

Plymouth Rock, claimed by those fleeing injustice,
as they saw it, religious persecution which they,
in turn, inflicted more visciously on those
who couldn't flee their own land, forever corrupted.

Berlin, Hilter fantasizing racial superiority,
foisting blame on one tribe, not his own,
pillaging, imprisoning, murdering, all he could
six million decimated, those surviving, lost.

Charlottesville, a peaceful march against tyranny
that threatens to alter what little equality exists
that preys on the poor, the coat of many colors we have
that ruined the peace, that murdered for hate.

Atlanta, Boulder, seething with grief and fear
that angry, little white men breed within
their narrow, scarred brains, as they act out hate
by a culture immured by its own warped beginnings.

Christmas Eve 2020

The year ends at midnight
one week from today.

I say, let's burn the plague of
this year's assault on decency

and compassion by hatred's disfiguring,
dislocation of our moral center.

Death to all tyrants, we once said,
as we became that which we disclaimed,

throwing the tea, loading the guns,
doing to others in the same vein.

The pestilence came for them disguised
as offerings of peace and goodwill.

The pestilence came for us disguised
as our neighbor, our father, our friend.

We must ignite this nightmare year so
the sparks of hope rise up, phoenix-like

from the flames, nourished by mercy,
by *caritas,* by *humanitas*, to all a good night.

Once upon a life

The smell of sauerkraut and potatoes
fills my small house and takes me back
in time to my mother cooking in her kitchen,
her Swedish-German heritage stirring within her
and into her food—brot, kuchen, sauerkraut—
a direct descent of dishes from mother to mother.

I think about them today as I make this comfort
food and the salty sour headiness of kraut mixes
with caraway, black pepper, potatoes, butter
filling the air and carrying me to a simpler time,
at least for a child. Then I consider my own
children whose lives were not simple even though
nurtured by this same comfort food.

Will they make brot and kuchen and kraut with joy?
Will they have a home filled with comfort and care?
Will a particular scent recall a happy memory of home?

Self- preservation

What will happen to all of it,
the paraphernalia of my life saved
over decades in a chest of cedar—
cards of birth, death, and love,
grandma's crocheted baby booties
baby teeth, children's art, letters,
pictures, old movie tickets, all the
bits and bobs of remembrances?
When I am gone will someone
cherish these or chastise me *in absentia*?

Will the cards my father, my mother inscribed
for birthdays, Christmases long past remain?
Will my grandmother's diaries, her well-thumbed
bible with fading cover survive?
Will my children's baby teeth, their infant art,
grandchildren's offerings of love be tossed or treasured?
Will these material remnants of me survive
my material demise when I shuffle off?

Shadowboxing with cancer

Cancer stalks me as it lurks in the shadows of my
life like the creature from my childish nightmares

that waited while I, wandering, searching every room
for help, felt its presence in the dark corners, like cobwebs.

Now, I wake from sleep not always from dreams and rise
to tend the business of aging night, but it follows me

from room to room, sits with me as I try not to think,
threatens me a third time, mocks my future hopes.

mæskə reɪd

I

The mask that hides his face
as he sleeps on the sand, in the
cooling shade of the palm, well-used
cloth that it is, hides his shame,
his anger, or his nonchalance at his
homeless state of being as the tourists
stroll by, picnic in the grass, swim
in the wealth of Waikiki.

II

"It's a fish. Deal with it," the short man
growled at the two women on the beach walk,
not obstructing, only admiring the little fish
swimming along the sea wall. The women saw
the angry, thwarted, impotent man beneath
his mask of misogyny and attitude, and sighed.
His inept attempt at belittling humiliation blown off
and away from them like the Trades along their
sunset stroll to mai tais and simple pleasures near the sea,
unknown to a wrath-filled, small-minded man
of sad character.

III

The local men came with smiles and apologies
for the intrusion. They will stop the leak of overstressed,
artificial air meant to cool haole sensitivity to tropic
heat. But, first, the pudgy, haole manager's undeserving ego
must be gratified, soothed by consultation though he knows
not what he does. An oversized white man strides in with booming
voice announcing, "I am the Owner." Manager man shrinks
bodily, his arrogant remarks and smirks at the working men
dying in his throat. But now, those men, trying to do the job,
must negotiate the bodies and bombast of two who

could not do what they must do to restore the balance
of this unnatural space.

IV

The darker-skinned native fishes bubble at the surface
picking at the debris tossed, lost, discarded by human excess
and disregard for life that's not their own. Nearby, a lone
angel fish shimmers just under the surface before
she dives to poke and prod the unnatural reef of concrete,
puzzled as to why it gives up so little sustenance. A puffer
glides beneath her, cautious, dangerous, nearly obscured
by the clutter of broken plastic, dirty tennis balls, swirls
of engine oil, wasters' detritus, the sticks and stones
of modern Hawaii.

Aprilis agon

Dante's April began with a descent through the circles of Hell
but Chaucer's incited "folk to gon on pilgrimages" while Shakespeare's
"proud-pied" April left a lover in the throes of winter, bereft of beauty,
alone, as Eliot's "cruellest month" devastated in a wasted land.

Our April, nearing its end, uncovers many faces of humankind
in a tragic comedy where clerics draw crowds to gasping death,
in a tale of folk, unsteadfast, bemused, confounded, in
a lament for beauty unremarked, of life played in shadow, in
a well-turned verse of regret, despair, and sad complacency.

Are we ready now to appease Nature's vengeance, her revenge
for our cruelty to our Mother before She cracks and excretes
countless unearned deaths, until we turn back to dust returning
to her once more, purified, cleansed, refreshed by April showers.

About the Author

In her former life as a professor of medieval and early modern English literature and creative writing, Julie Chappell published six books of scholarship, including the monograph *Perilous Passages: The Book of Margery Kempe, 1534-1934* (Palgrave 2013) and the collection of scholarly essays, *Bad Girls and Transgressive Women in Popular Television, Fiction, and Film* (Palgrave 2017) co-edited with Dr. Mallory Young. She also read her creative works widely in a variety of venues in California, Kansas, Texas, and Oklahoma, among other locations, winning the Grand Slam Poetry Prize in Lawrence, Kansas in 1994. Her poetry and prose have appeared in several anthologies and journals including *Revival: Spoken Word from Lollapalooza 94*; *Agave: A Celebration of Tequila in Story, Song, Poetry, Essay, and Graphic Art*; *Elegant Rage: A Poetic Tribute to Woody Guthrie*; *The Call of the Chupacabra*; *Malpaïs Review*; *Voices de la Luna*; *Concho River Review*; *Stone Renga*; *Speak Your Mind: Woody Guthrie Poets Celebrate Freedom of Speech 2019, Poems of Protest & Resistance*; and *Bull Buffalo and Indian Paintbrush (The Poetry of Oklahoma)*. Her first collection of short fiction, *Homecoming and Other Mythic Tales*, was published by Fine Dog Press in July 2021. She has two other collections of original poetry—*Faultlines: One Woman's Shifting Boundaries* (Village Books Press, 2013) and *Mad Habits of a Life* (Lamar University Literary Press, 2019) which was nominated for the Paterson Poetry Prize in 2020. *As I Pirouette Away* is her third collection of original poetry.

www.ingramcontent.com/pod-product-compliance
Lightning Source LLC
Chambersburg PA
CBHW081158070526
44583CB00021B/2898